THE SAILORS OF ULM

OTHER POETRY BOOKS BY ANDY CROFT

Nowhere Special (Flambard, 1996)

Gaps Between Hills (Scratch, 1996) with Dermot Blackburn and Mark Robinson

Letter to Randall Swingler (Shoestring, 1999)

Just as Blue (Flambard, 2001)

Headland (Scratch, 2001) with Dermot Blackburn

Great North (IRON Press, 2001)

Comrade Laughter (Flambard, 2004)

Ghost Writer (Five Leaves, 2007)

Sticky (Flambard, 2009)

Three Men on the Metro (Five Leaves, 2009) with W.N. Herbert and Paul Summers

1948 (Five Leaves, 2012) with Martin Rowson

A Modern Don Juan: Cantos for these Times by Divers Hands (Five Leaves, 2014) with N.S. Thompson *et al*

Les éléphants de Mudfog (Les Temps des Cerises, 2016)

Letters to Randall Swingler (Shoestring, 2017)

THE SAILORS OF ULM

ANDY CROFT

Shoestring Press

Printed by imprintdigital
Upton Pyne, Exeter
www.digital.imprint.co.uk

Typesetting by narrator
www.narrator.me.uk
info@narrator.me.uk
033 022 300 39

Published by Shoestring Press
19 Devonshire Avenue, Beeston, Nottingham, NG9 1BS
(0115) 925 1827
www.shoestringpress.co.uk

First published 2020
© Copyright: Andy Croft
© Cover by Martin Rowson (after Gerricault)

The moral right of the author has been asserted.

ISBN 978-1-912524-48-8

ACKNOWLEDGMENTS

Thanks are due to the editors of the following publications where some of these poems first appeared: *Al-Hilal* (Egypt), *Bain an-nahrain* (Iraq), *The Black Light Engine Room*, *Kuzbass XXI Century* (Russia), *Markings*, *Mistress Quickly's Bed*, *The Morning Star*, *The New European*, *The Nordic Journal of English Studies*, *The North*, *Penniless Press*, *Poetry Salzburg Review*, *Race and Class* and *Zone Sensible* (Paris).

Others were first published in *Time in the Shape of a Mine: Poems from Combe Down* (2009); Bob Beagrie *et al* (eds), *How Things are Made: Poems for Gordon Hodgeon* (2009); Alan Morrison (ed), *The Robin Hood Book* (2013); Edward Carvalho (ed), *The Acknowledged Legislator* (2014); Andy Croft and NS Thompson (eds), *A Modern Don Juan* (2014); Neil Fulwood and David Sillitoe (eds), *More Raw Material: work inspired by Alan Sillitoe (2015);* Annie Wright *et al* (eds), *Northbound* (2016); Amarjit Chandan *et al* (eds), *The Long White Thread of Words: Poems for John Berger (*2016); James Walker (ed), *Dawn of the Unread (*2016); Francis Combes (ed), *Les éléphants de Mudfog* (Paris, 2016); Merryn Williams (ed), *Strike Up The Band* (2017).

An early version of 'Massacre' was commissioned by the Poetry Society for the Tate Gallery website TATE ETC. 'Gathering' was commissioned by the Newcastle May Day march in 2009. 'The Work of Giants' and 'The Last Act of Harry Patch' were commissioned by the Combe Down Stone Mines Project in Bath. 'Moving Backwards' was commissioned by Northern Architecture to accompany guided tours of historical Middlesbrough. 'The Apollo Pavilion: A Concrete Poem' was commissioned by Durham County Council. 'Cider in their Ears' was written for the memorial meeting in Sheffield celebrating the life of the writer and radio-producer Dave Sheasby.

in memory of Gordon Hodgeon

'Can we be sure that, if the fall had only crippled the tailor instead of killing him, he would have immediately picked himself up and tried again, or that his friends would not have tried to restrain him? And what contribution did his bold attempt actually make to the history of aeronautics?'

– Lucio Magri

CONTENTS

THE SAILORS OF ULM

for Tim

Put out to sea, my broken comrades,
Unfurl the torn and tattered hearts
Tattooed upon our fading colours,
For though the seas have all run dry
And our boats burned, and all our charts
Forgot, we'll get there by and by.

Run up the sail, my heartsick comrades,
The tide has turned, all hands on deck,
Let all who sail this lunar ocean
Recall the faithful crew who drowned
Inside the bleached whale of our wreck
When, rudderless, we run aground.

Don't rock the boat, ignoble comrades,
Or we might end up in the drink.
Our course is set. On the horizon
The sun is setting. On the quay
The rats are cheering as we sink
Beneath the sands. We're all at sea.

MASSACRE

for John Berger at ninety

after André Fougeron's Massacre de Sakiet III

How well we know these careless faces—
The children smiling in their sleep,
The ecstasy of death's embraces,
The naked girl thrown on a heap
Of awkward limbs and broken bodies.
The trophied heads. The silent squaddies.
We were not there the day the skies
Fell in, and yet we recognise
These peaceful and civilian features
So well we barely catch our breath;
Who are so intimate with death
We know these killings barely reach us;
But most of all we know whose boots
Stand guarding over empire's fruits.

This knowledge must be classified
So you and I can sleep at night,
And five-year olds, once pacified
By bombs, must be hushed out of sight
By spokesmen with imperial smiles.
How well we know their smooth denials
And how they help us understand
Such deaths as these are never planned,
But air-strikes cost the tax-payer millions,
And if our aims are imprecise,
Then somebody must pay the price:
This shrouded crowd of dead civilians
Who look at us as if to say
They will not let us look away.

Since these were murdered in Tunisia
Collateral damage is the norm.
Since '58 Death's gotten busier;
From Shock and Awe to Desert Storm
Our wars are won by air-offensive;
In PR terms it's less expensive—
More bangs for bucks, more flesh per pound—
Than putting boots in on the ground.
And so the dead are always nameless,
Uncounted, slaughtered in a war
By enemies they never saw,
And we, whose dreams are always blameless,
Lie listening for the noiseless drone
Of desert whirlwinds we have sown.

THE GREAT BELL IN MARTÍN ESPADA'S CHEST

'You got a song, man, sing it.
You got a bell, man, ring it.'
Robert Creeley

'The moon is the tongue
In the bell of the sky.'
Sergei Esenin

It was after the Liverpool reading
    As we walked back towards the hotel,
Though he tried not to show it, the visiting poet
    Was suddenly feeling unwell.

Perhaps he was suffering from jet lag,
    Or maybe he needed a rest,
But down Penny Lane, he began to complain
    Of a sharp ringing pain in his chest.

At the hospital, none of the doctors
    Could explain what the problem might be,
So he said where it hurt and they took of his shirt
    And they tapped him three times on each knee.

Then they measured and prodded and weighed him
    From his beard to the soles of his feet,
But his arteries pumped, and his heart-beat still thumped
    (On the left side, where all hearts should beat).

Since he seemed in such good working order
    The doctors could hardly explain
Why this model of fitness (as God was their witness),
    Should be in such terrible pain.

But before they could safely discharge him,
    They decided to do one more test,
But all they could see from a quick ECG
    Was what looked like—a bell in his chest!

Within minutes a team of consultants
    Were stood at the foot of his bed,
'It's impossible surely—no wonder he's poorly,
    By rights this man ought to be dead.'

It was all in the next morning's papers
    'POET FOUND WITH A BELL IN HIS CHEST!'
'Is he clapped out or cracked? Is he freakish or fact?
    Monster placed under cardiac arrest!'

Well they needed more time to establish
    Where the bell in his rib-cage was from,
So they called in the Law so they could be quite sure
    That the bell wasn't really a bomb.

Then the government launched an inquiry
    To allay any public unrest;
The inquiry was clear there was nothing to fear
    From a man with a bell in his chest:

'This is not the long-lost bell of Bosham,
    Or the bell that's beneath Comber Mere,
Or the bell which the rat thought to put on the cat,
    Or the one from the *Santa Maria*;

'It possesses no military value,
    And investors aren't likely to pay
Just to sponsor a chime that cannot tell the time
    And does not call the faithful to pray;

'We conclude that this bell is quite useless,
        Its commercial potential is small,
And it's only perhaps if we melt it for scrap
        It will have any value at all;

'We propose, in the interests of science,
        To cut out the great bell with a knife,
Though there is a slight risk (the report here was brisk)
        That it might cost the patient his life.'

Although previously patient, the patient
        Now opened his mouth to protest,
And the sound which came out was an eloquent shout
        And it rang like a bell in his chest;

It was loud as a shirt from Hawaii,
        It was deep as a bell lost at sea,
And it rolled its long tongue round a carillon song
        That was ringing to set the world free;

And it rose like a wave in the ocean,
        And it echoed the hopes of the years
Like an ancient dry well or a green broken bell,
        And it swelled like a chorus of tears;

And it rang for the weak and the hungry,
        And it sang for the poor and oppressed,
And all those who bear violence with patience and silence,
        Forgetting the bell in their chest.

Though the world may be heavy and hollow,
        It can ring out as poetry does,
But don't ask why it rolls or for whom the bell tolls—
        When it's singing for each one of us.

PAUL ROBESON SINGS IN MUDFOG TOWN HALL

for Gordon

'And upon his hip was a double edged sword
And his mouth was a gospel horn.'
'Joshua Fought the Battle of Jericho'

'The message in my music is that all men are brothers.'
Paul Robeson, *Evening Gazette*, 22 April 1960

And when at last they gave his passport back
    He made a tour of Northern small town halls,
Still handsome, clever, radical and black,
    His voice still strong enough to shake the walls.
But though the place was packed, the three front-rows
    (Reserved for all the local great and good)
Were pointedly unoccupied by those
    Apparently afraid of brotherhood.
Though no-one who was anyone was there,
    The no-ones who are everybody came—
The nobodies who know that everywhere
    There's somebody who thinks they're not the same,
As if there's anybody could delay
The walls of privilege tumbling down one day.

MOVING BACKWARDS

*'Weeds and rust, rust and weeds! I can imagine a party of antiquarians a
hundred years hence exploring the ruins of the extinct town and observing to
one another that the world had not lost very much by its disappearance.'*
Douglas Goldring, writing about Middlesbrough in 1925

1

The first step is the most important
(Plato's *Republic*, see Book II)
Or you might end up where you oughtn't—
As towns like this so often do.
This lyric fountain outside mima's
A hazard for unwary dreamers,
So watch your step as we re-trace
The steps that brought us to this place.
For those who're always Moving Forward
This is a chance to learn the knack
Of turning round and walking back
The way we came, by heading shoreward
And putting History in reverse.
That is, we're going from bad to worse.

2

From bad to worse? Such condescension
Sounds rather like we're tempting fate;
These days, despite our best intentions,
Tomorrow's always out of date;
And if we think the past unpleasant,
What should we say about the present?
We need a Virgil (or Ian Stubbs)
To point out that these clubs and pubs
On Albert Road in former ages
Are where the town once kept its cash;
Now Friday nights, out on the lash,
The town comes here to spend its wages.
The banks, of course, don't think it strange,
And no-one stops to counts the change.

3

Because we do not have a TARDIS
To take us back, we'll have to walk,
And as we do, we'll try our hardest
To let the architecture talk
Above the roar of passing traffic
(It might help if you're telepathic)
Above us on the A66.
This road is like the River Styx—
On this side is the living present,
On that, the kingdom of the Dead
Whose emblem is this severed head.
On Zetland Place the Bath-like crescent
Stares vacantly, as if to say
Abandon hope, who pass this way.

4

A town is more than bricks and mortar,
We all need beauty, hope and art—
Which brings us to the Cultural Quarter,
Where web-designers get to start
What Webb & Company once finished.
With optimism undiminished
We start again. And then once more,
As though we've not been here before.
We're climbing now, to old St Hilda's,
Up Cleveland Street, towards the sky.
Here ancient buildings come to die,
Like monuments to all the builders
Whose every bright new start succeeds
The last in fields of rust and weeds.

5

On Tower Green we've reached the summit
Of our ambition. After this
It's all down hill. Before we plummet
Down Durham Street we almost miss
The market square once sketched by Lowry.
Graffiti tags grow wild and flowery
Like tattoos round the old Town Hall;
Although the writing's on the wall
We don't know how to read the data—
Some runic language which consists
Of dates and names in scribbled lists
(As least this gives it *listed* status!)
Perhaps if we could read these signs
We'd understand how *urbs* declines.

6

When Gladstone spoke, the world was younger,
And Hercules was just a boy.
Hard labour, enterprise and hunger—
We worship what we next destroy;
The work's now blown away like litter;
These days he's working as a fitter
Somewhere down south. Come Saturday
He's back to watch the Boro play.
The seasons pass in desperation,
Slow moving as tectonic plates.
On match-days through the turnstile gates,
We count the cost of relegation,
The levelled history of a town
That's strongest when it gets knocked down.

7

We've time to catch the karaoke
Just starting at the Captain Cook.
Though not as busy (or as smoky)
As once it was, it's worth a look.
Inside, a century slowly passes
As thirsty ghosts re-fill their glasses.
Peg Powler sometimes drinks in here.
She knows all this will disappear
One day, just like the old Transporter,
This bridge that links the transmundane
To re-runs of *Auf Wiedersehen*.
I asked her once what life had taught her
Among the lowest of the dead.
She finished off her pint and said:

8

The first step is the most important,
So watch your step and don't tempt fate
Or you might end up where you oughtn't.
Hard labour isn't out of date.
We knew that when the world was younger.
Ambition, enterprise and hunger
Are strongest when you get knocked down;
The levelled history of this town
Is all down hill and moving forward;
And if the writing's on the wall
Like tattoos round the old Town Hall,
The signs are that we're heading shoreward
To start again, and then once more,
As though we've not been here before...

THE APOLLO PAVILION: A CONCRETE POEM

'an architecture and sculpture of purely abstract form through which to walk,
in which to linger and on which to play, a free and anonymous monument
which, because of its independence, can lift the activity and psychology of an
urban housing community on to a universal plane.'
Victor Pasmore

In Peterlee the new town plan
A bright pavilion did decree
For those who dug the coal that ran
In caverns measureless to man
    Beneath the cold North Sea.

They named it for the gods whom we
Watched orbit round the night's balloon
Like sailors on a tranquil sea,
Until it seemed that Peter Lee
    Was really the man in the moon.

One small step for a man, all right,
A giant leap for us to follow
Whose concrete boots cannot take flight;
A shrine to art and truth and light
    In honour of Apollo.

It marks the ends of our ambition
Who thought the future once had wings
From Xanadu to Saturn mission,
A monument to the condition
    Of all unfinished things.

The law that says the best laid schemes
Unravel just as they begin,
Turns those who sink their deepest dreams
In caves of ice or coal-hot seams
    To enemies within.

The footprints on those lunar seas
Lead all the way downhill to Porlock
And back again. Now Peterlee's
Where *Life is Cheap* and *Death is Free*'s
    The wisdom of the Morlock.

The future is a savage place
Which sunlit art can scarcely warm;
We scribble in the margin's space
Our discontents—a concrete case
    Of content over form,

And hope that History isn't done,
That maybe in the bye and bye
We'll finish what was once begun,
And orbiting around the sun
    Teach concrete how to fly.

GATHERING

for Chris at 70

When I woke in this city one fine May Day morning
    I saw a small crowd, like a gathering stream,
And though they were only a few hundred strong,
They were singing old songs I'd not heard for so long
    That it seemed I was still in a dream.

'O where are you going this fine May Day morning?
    And what are these flags that you carry so bright?'
'We are marching,' they said, 'in the steps of the dead,
Of all those who have marched under banners of red,
    So that we may continue their fight'.

'But why are you angry this fine May Day morning,
    When the Summer is wearing its holiday hat?'
'We are angry,' they said, 'that the people must pay
With their jobs and their homes for the world's disarray
    While the rich and the powerful grow fat.'

'But what can you do on this fine May Day morning?
    When their lies are so many and you are so few?'
'Our strength' they replied, 'is not measured in numbers,
For our songs have awoken the dead from their slumbers.'
    And I listened and knew it was true.

For I heard in the crowd on this fine May Day morning
    The voices of those who had marched here before:
In the fight for the Charter, for Land and for Bread,
For the Eight-Hour Day, for the Haymarket dead,
    For the victims of hunger and war;

They were marching from Sedgemoor, from Newport and Burford,
    They came from Soweto and Moscow and Spain,
And they carried their flags from Hanoi and Havana
Till it seemed that the city was one scarlet banner
    And it shone like a glittering plain.

And I watched as they marched on this fine May Day morning,
    Like a field full of folk by the banks of the Tyne,
As strong as a river that reaches the sea,
As old as the rings in a blossoming tree,
    And I saw that their banners were mine.

ADULT EDUCATION CLASSES, 1980S

for Allan

The 1930s. Mansfield. Monday nights.
We're studying the Spanish Civil War,
When those who tried to put the world to rights
Were taught that freedom's always premature.

The 1980s. Ashfield. Day-release.
An NUM Communications course
For those whose eloquence can't match the force
Of lying press and militarised police.

Today the struggle is an ancient text
In which we trace the victory march of violence
From one dishonest decade to the next;
The best are always beaten into silence,
Defeated still by education, class,
And History still shrugs, and says Alas.

THE WORK OF GIANTS

'as though they had been the rocks fabled to have been piled up by the giants against heaven, and then hurled down by the thunder of Jupiter.'
John Wood

'Let Nature never be forgot'
Alexander Pope

O Happiness! Our being's end and aim!
Good, Pleasure, Ease, Content! Whate'er the name
We seek when we give up our native hearth—
The traveller's Holy Grail lies here in Bath
(Or B*a*th as I would call it, since my mouth
Must flatten vowels they dwell on in the South).
But whether you're from North, South, East or West,
This town's the end of every pilgrim's quest,
A Mecca where the waiters at your table
All speak the international tongue of Babel,
A coach-tour operator's Shangri-la,
A place to take the waters, see the Spa
And worship at the temple of Jane Austen.
We flock from Sydney, Tokyo and Boston
And every distant corner of the earth
(Like Bennet *filles* pursuing Colin Firth);
We circle round these honeyed Squares and Crescents
Collecting tea-towel souvenirs as presents,
Meander round Palladian colonnades
And marvel at the Circles and Parades
Whose fame (thanks to the blessings of UNESCO)
Might now be said to almost rival Tesco.
        Before our coach departs for Hadrian's Wall,
(Or was that yesterday?) we might recall
The eighteenth-century men who built this town
With oolithic limestone from Combe Down—
The masons and the quarrymen whose sweat
Helped built this Nash-ville costume-drama set,
The unrecorded hands that raised the stones
Which we have just recorded on our phones.

17

So while we knock back lattes by the gallon
Let's think about the Woods and low-born Allen
Who with, as Pope once said, 'an awkward shame'
Did 'good by stealth and blushed to find it fame'—
The kind of patron Pope could not resist,
Though adding with the usual spiteful twist,
If 'virtue choose the high or low degree,
Tis all alike to virtue, and to me.'
But virtue—like degree—is just a label
We use to make the world seem less unstable,
And high and low alike need others' labours
To build the walls which join us to our neighbours;
Society needs more than bricks and mortar
Or else our lives are nasty, brute and shorter.
So let us pause between the weary stops
Of fudge, fridge-magnet, cake and coffee shops
To look up from our dog-eared A-Zs
And wonder at the stones above our heads.

      The Anglo-Saxons—whom we might record
As tourist pioneers—were also awed
By what they found in Bath: the plundered walls,
Fate-shattered towers, the splendid ruined halls
They thought were built by giants, long departed.
It never took them much to get them started
On gloomy thoughts regarding earth's embrace,
But here in Bath they found the ruined face
Of stone an emblem of the world's decay,
The brightness and the shortness of our day
Who rise up, Babel-like, before we fall
Age-eaten as a mossy Roman wall.

      Just like, perhaps, the tiny, ocean creatures
Who gave Bath Stone its now distinctive features
200 million years ago (approx.).
The strata that we know as Egg-stone rocks
Were slowly formed by dead siphonophores
Upon some dark Jurassic ocean floors;
Their memory's now carved in Combe Down stone,
As soft as flesh and frangible as bone,
And yet more durable than human clay,

18

A monument to *change* and not decay.

     Appropriate for Ralph Allen, whom tradition
Remembers as a man of quiet ambition,
Whose meteoric rags-to-riches rise
Mixed public works and private enterprise,
Who rose from humble-born post-office clerk,
To be the master-builder of Prior Park,
A show-house built to be a mansion fit
For guests like Fielding, Richardson and Pitt.
Although he made his fortune shifting stones
He was the living model in *Tom Jones*
For Allworthy, that model English Squire
Whose modest worth all readers can admire.
He built this house in Combe Down by decree
'To see all Bath and for all Bath to see'—
The proper doctrine of a self-made man
Whose modesty's on view for all to scan.
To treat the Goddess 'like a modest fair
Not over-dress, nor leave her wholly bare'
Was Pope's advice to those who had the lolly
To rusticate their gardens with a folly
(Imagine what the Anglo-Saxon mind
Would make of ruins purposely designed!)
If bare, unfinished Nature were removed
Pope thought the natural world would be improved,
Hence all these 'wildernesses', water-falls
And Roman-temple film-set ruined walls
Designed to make the landscaped Georgian mansion
Seen natural as strict iambic scansion.

     Although it's rather long for 2K9,
I've tried to use this plodding five beat line
To gently mock the mock-heroic trope
Much used by mates of Allen's, such as Pope—
A stately form, Augustan and ornate,
Ideal for poets who wish to cultivate
Their betters (and to part them from their dosh).
Although it isn't subtle, it sounds posh,
A classical Baroque and roll back-beat
That dances to the beat of Latin feet

By claiming London as a second Rome
(Like flipping MP's claim a second home).
Though to your face it's decorous and pretty,
Behind the pose of being cool and witty
The low-born writer has sufficient freedom
To gently bite the high-born hands that feed 'em,
An English picturesque designed to trick us—
Like statues of Diana with no knickers.

Although the National Trust runs Prior Park
Ralph Allen's house is now, we may remark,
A public school, which means the private grounds
Are to the paying public out of bounds.
From China to the West Bank and Berlin
Strong walls keep people out as well as in.
A wall can be a shelter or a line
Designed to demarcate your world from mine,
A party-wall, or one built to divide us
By separating locals from outsiders.
'Beyond the pale' (from Roman *palus* 'stake')
Is still employed to talk of those who break
The rules that we design to maintain order.

Combe Down has always functioned as a border:
The Wansdyke (ie Woden's ditch) describes
The front line held between the Saxon tribes.
From Anglo-Saxon 'dunun' meaning 'hill'
And 'cumbe' (a vale), this little place is still
Both high and low, above/below, between,
A typically English village scene;
The little patch that gave us Harry Patch
And *Danny Boy*. Between them these two catch
Our sense of something lost beyond recalling,
The Summer gone and all the roses falling.
The Titfield line was closed by Beeching's axe
The Post Office by economic facts,
And deep beneath the surface of the mind
This England has been slowly undermined
By centuries of digging in the dark.
While Allen took the stone to Prior Park
And Nash's Bath rose up towards the light

The deepest truths were buried out of sight.
    You do not need to read the works of Freud
To know the Natural world abhors a void
Or that the past is never really closed.
'Whatever is, is Right,' Pope once proposed,
Assuming that in Nature he would find
A model for the laws of humankind;
And so he did, of course, by the appliance
Of some—ahem—extremely dodgy science
In which the Laws of Nature seemed to be
Less interested in virtue, than degree.
    Let's hear it for the miners then, who braved
The tunnel-dark that Combe Down might be saved;
The low-born Sons of Wales who left their homes
To crawl among these stone-mine honeycombs,
And Atlas-like hold up the earth's foundations
Worn Doric-thin by previous generations;
The enemy within whose lives remind us
That History is standing just behind us,
That what goes round must one day come around,
Like gaping voids beneath the daily ground.
We put back what we take or else we face
The pressure of the planet's hard embrace,
Then high and low will all go to the wall,
And all the stone-built works of giants fall.

THE LAST ACT OF HARRY PATCH

His murder was arranged at Ypres
With half a million other men,
But now he's dead, the simpering vipers
Come crawling out from Number 10
To bury him with loud laudation
And hymns to reconciliation—
The poisonous, forked-tongued response
Of those who tried to kill him once,
Who justify each round of killing
From Langemarck to Afghanistan,
Then shed a tear for one old man.
It's hard to say which is more chilling.
These snakes are deaf to what he said.
There's nothing else. And now he's dead.

TOMSKAYA PISANITSA PARK, KEMEROVO

for Dasha

'we all matter, we are all indelible, miraculous, here.'
Julia Darling

1

We take a break from our discussions
About the British poetry scene.
About time too; I've bored these Russians
Quite long enough now. In between
Each post-New Gen New Generation
And last week's latest new sensation,
I have the sense they're not impressed.
Oh dear. Although I've tried my best,
When every poet is 'dark' and 'daring',
Each new collection 'vibrant', 'bold',
And last year's new is this year's old,
The sum effect is somewhat wearing.
There's rather more to art, I fear,
Than simply saying, *I was here.*

2

We take the bus across the river.
Beneath the wide Kuznetsky Bridge
They're fishing on the ice. We shiver.
It would be warmer in a fridge.
We're driving North, past roadside diners,
The monument to Kuzbass miners,
The forest blur of greys and browns,
And summer-dacha shantytowns,
Scalectrix roads and lego churches.
The bus slows down. At last we're there.
We stop among the silent glare
And tinsel glitter of the birches
(I borrowed this line from a verse
By Mandelshtam—it could be worse).

3

Ten minutes later, we're stood gazing
In frozen silence at these cliffs—
A frieze of hundreds of amazing
Six thousand year old petroglyphs
That stretch from Dürer-like cross hatches
To etch-a-sketchish childish scratches.
Abraded, nicked and tricked and picked,
These scrawls upon the walls depict
A pre-Deluvian procession
Of aurochs, foxes, wolves and deer,
A hunter with a pointy spear
(Or bandy-stick). Sod self-expression—
It seems to me all art starts from
These pictograms beside the Tom.

4

The Sympathetic Magic thesis
(See Abbé Breuil, of Lascaux fame)
Proposed that it was through mimesis
That we first taught ourselves to name
And tame the growling world with patterns;
That art expands the things it flattens;
That humankind first found its tongue
When rhythmic gesture, dance and song
Marked out the grunter from the grunting;
That knocking matter into shape's
What separates us from the apes;
And that the hunted started hunting
When we began to imitate
Creation's hunger on a plate.

5

Imagined goals are scored by winners—
Once caught by art upon these rocks
These animals were Sunday dinners,
A winter coat, a pair of socks.
No need to shiver by the river
When art's enchantments can deliver
A woolly vest to keep you warm.
A pelt fits like a well-made form,
A birthday suit (but less informal),
A fur-lined cloak in which to hide
And keep the hungry world outside,
A second skin that feels, well, normal.
In short, when we first borrowed fur,
The human soup began to stir.

6

The world out there is strange and formless,
A wilderness of blood and force—
Art's job's to make it seem less gormless
(From *gaumr*, 'lacking sense'—Old Norse).
These primitive caricaturists
Were never art-for-art's-sake purists;
Their work was useful as an axe,
Each rock-engraving made the facts
Of Neolithic dreams still bigger.
Above the bison, bears and birds
The stick-men chasing reindeer herds,
There seems to be a flying figure
Among the stars and solar rings:
A human with a pair of wings.

7

Cue Kubrik's famous match-cut edit
As trumpets fanfare to the dawn:
A handy tool with which to credit
The narrative of brain and brawn
(An always useful combination)
That saw us conquer all creation
And take our place among the stars.
Leonov's weightless boots were *ours*.
But you can't space-walk like a model
Or take your partner in the waltz
Unless you know which steps are false;
Before a child can learn to toddle.
As someone said, you need the knack
Of sometimes taking one step back.

8

This Kemerovo conurbation
Was built by US Reds with dreams;
They came at Lenin's invitation
To drain the coal-rich Kuzbass seams
Which Kolchak's Whites had lately flooded,
They stayed four years, and worked and studied
Till Comrade One-Crutch learned to fly
And Big Bill Heywood's good left eye
Could see that they had half-created
A Wobblie city in the sticks.
And then, in 1926,
The colony was 'liquidated',
Historians wiped the record clean,
Almost as if they'd never been.

9

Just like the old Siberian Yeti
Whose hairy footprints in the snow
Get journalists all hot and sweaty
At forty-five degrees below;
Though sightings are reported yearly
The cynics say that they are merely
A troupe of circus bruins who
Escaped from some old Soviet zoo,
Deciding that unspoken freedom
Sounds better than the world's applause.
The Park's bears, meanwhile, show their claws
To Sunday visitors who feed 'em
Their honeyed wages through the bars
That separates their world from ours.

10

In Bear Rock cave a single finger
Is all that's left of some lost race
Who lacked, perhaps, the art to linger
Before they vanished without trace;
Perhaps they never learned to fashion
The world to get their morning ration;
Or else they lacked the wherewithal
To read the writing on the wall
That spelled out their abrupt extinction.
These folk were here. And now they've gone.
Like sabre-tooth and mastodon.
The hungry world makes no distinction
Between the beasts on which we prey
And those to which we used to pray.

11

But evidence of evolution's
A kind of messy palimpsest—
These rocks include some contributions
By later artists (*Ya bil zdes*)—
To wit, although we think we're brainier
We can't shake off the graphomania
We caught six thousand years ago
(Like writers pissing in the snow).
These bare rocks mark the clumsy stages
By which we make our slow ascent;
All art can do is represent
Our progress on their uncut pages
Asserting that we all were here
Before we each must disappear.

MISHA

There once was a bear,
A flea-bitten bear,
Who lived all alone in the wood;
And he lay in bed all winter long,
And he slept, as all bears should.

And while he slept,
This flea-bitten bear,
He dreamed of flaxen heads,
Of empty bowls and broken chairs
And children burned in their beds.

And when he woke,
That flea-bitten bear,
The snows began to melt,
But nothing could thaw the Winter's dream
Or the loneliness he felt.

Beyond the cave
Of that flea-bitten bear
The forest was dark and dim,
And everywhere the bear did go,
The Winter followed him.

Pursued by dreams,
That flea-bitten bear,
Of twenty million dead,
He lay awake, afraid to sleep,
Alone in his bear-skin bed.

And late at night,
That flea-bitten bear,
When he hears the dark attack,
He roars and growls, he barks and he howls.
And the Winter answers back.

FEARFUL SYMMETRY

for Sheree

'Each has a gift that Nature gave,
But some their neighbour's fame must crave.'
Ivan Krylov

The lion shakes its regal mane,
The monkey thumps his chest,
The narwhal waves its tusk, the crab his claws;
The peacock flaunts its gorgeous train,
The bowerbird his nest,
The civet sprays her musk, the tiger roars,
As they will:
Creation on the catwalk's dressed to kill.

What artist's palette 'ere revealed
 Such bright and vivid hues?
What hand or eye could frame such drop-dead threads?
What cobbler's last has ever heeled
 So many fuck-me shoes?
This cattle-market game of turning heads
 Means your date
Is either your next meal or else your mate.

Alas, far from the critics' praise
There dwells Arachne's kin
Whose intricate designs go unrewarded;
Condemned by vain and boastful ways
To sit alone and spin
And know their silken lines are not applauded,
 Spiders must
Live out their days in realms of gloom and dust.

Frustrated by their dark estate,
The eight-legged tribe agreed
To give a special prize to Nature's spinners;
So others might appreciate
The art that spiders need,
They asked their friends the flies to crown the winners.
As it does,
The teeming insect world began to buzz.

While waiting for the six-legged crowd
To hit the spiders' gala,
Each thought her own design beyond compare,
Original, authentic, proud—
But flies know that the parlour
Where spiders like to dine, that winding stair,
Leads us straight
To something that no art can imitate.

And so, while other creatures sing
And preen and prance and puff,
This cobweb crew are still the world's outsiders;
When artless Nature does its thing,
And struts its gorgeous stuff,
The little beady gaze of every spider's
Still on the prize,
In realms of dust and dark, still counting flies.

ARCHY SAYS HOORAY

boss i have heard
some human beans think
hungry and homeless people
are like cockroaches i
am flattered at
last some humans beans feel
sorry for us poor insects
hooray there is
hope for some human beans after
all either that or the
human beans who think
hungry and homeless people
are like cockroaches
are worse than
cockroaches we would
never be so unkind

archy

A BLESSED PLOT

'In the great bee crisis, it is impossible not to see the metaphor.'
Boris Johnson

As usual the flowers were complaining
About their blooming lot—
In Winter it was always raining,
The Summers were too hot,
The hedge too high;
The shrubbery and rose-beds needed weeding,
The edges cutting back,
The mossy lawn required reseeding,
The black-flies were too black,
The soil too dry.

But nothing bugged these flowers like the spectre
Of swarms of honey-bees
Who helped themselves to English nectar
And never once said please.
'Those striped marauders!'
'It's time we told the bees that we don't need 'em!'
And so they took a poll
And talked about the blossoming of freedom
Once they'd won back control
Of their own borders.

Next morning when the honey-bees clocked on
The flowers hid their faces,
Until the busy bees had gone
To find more friendly places
Than this sad grot.
Which now is left a bolted, blighted spot
Of rust and smut and weed,
A wilderness of inky blot,
A garden gone to seed
And left to rot.

Moral

The earth's the fruit of all our labours
    While Eve still spins and Adam delves,
And those who do not like their neighbours
    Must learn to go and fuck themselves.

THE SHEEP AND THE GOATS

'So why refuse a vote to wolves of good repute?'
Ivan Krylov

Behold—a happy, sylvan scene
Of meadows wild and tall,
Of thistles sharp and nettles green;
A well-fenced park
With grass enough for all;
Where goats and sheep could sleep at night
Far from the horrid tale
Of burning eyes and teeth that bite
In forests dark,
Out there beyond the pale.

Though there was field enough to share,
The fold was fouled, alas,
By ruminants who filled the air
With woolly bleating
About who owned the grass.
Each day the rivalry increased
Between the sheep and goats,
Who, thinking they were being fleeced,
Instead of eating
Were at each other's throats.

But then one night when all were sleeping
Behind the high-walled dyke,
A hungry silhouette came creeping
With dreams of hay
For sheep and goats alike;
It offered them both bigger shares
Of Nature's green estate,
And promised them it would be theirs
If only they
Would open up the gate.

Next day the creatures had no doubt
About what they should do:
The monsters they had dreamed about
Could use those claws
To make their dreams come true;
They'd lick their rivals into shape,
The other Bovid lot
Would not be able to escape
Those ripping jaws.
And what big teeth they've got!

Their choices made, the Caprine kin
Had barely cast their votes
Before the wolves came grinning in
And with a leap
Had seized them by their throats.
When Fascism is at the door
With promises of grass,
It doesn't matter whether you're
A goat or sheep—
Don't let the bastards pass.

A WILLIMANTIC FABLE

for Jon, Denise, Miles and Kit

after Dick Wilbur

There's none who heard that cry of midnight dread
    And infinite dismay
Could doubt that it was sent to wake the dead
    On Judgement Day.

    The warm New England air
Seemed swollen by a strange inhuman wail,
The feral song of things unknown, out there,
    Beyond the pale.

And as we listened to the murderous drumming
    Of savage, frenzied revels,
We knew it was an Indian army coming.
    Or else the Devil's.

    In every horrid groan
We saw our children dead, our farms in flames,
In every cry of bullet, blood and bone
    We heard our names.

Some fell upon the Mercy of the Lord
    To lead us through the night,
While others, armed with pitchfork, gun and sword,
    Prepared to fight.

    The dogs began to bark,
Our army readied for the first attack,
The bravest started shooting in the dark.
    But none fired back.

We watched all night. But when the stars were fled
        And day lit up the roads,
We saw no foreign army, but instead
            A host of toads.

        The alien sound of slaughter
Of savage judgement from the world beyond,
Was just some bullfrogs singing by the water
            In Windham pond.

        Moral

Of all the leaping terrors that draw near
        When we are in our beds
The greatest are the fears we hear
            Inside our heads.

The splendid heroes of the night
        Are fools in day's disgrace,
And our own fears the only fight
            We need to face.

SUNLIGHT ON VERMONT

for Laura, in memory of Frank

We buried the cat beneath the sky
    Where the trees begin, on top of the hill,
For the seasons insist that all creatures must die
    When they are ill.
And death must always have its fill.

He'd swallowed nine lives, and then some more,
    But never could stomach the idea that
We're none of us more than tooth and claw.
    Though death grows fat
There's more than one way to skin a cat.

The days now grow both dark and cold
    And earth is turning widdershins,
But if you look beneath the trees, the old
    Blue Cat still grins
On top of the hill, where the sky begins.

PLAY IT AGAIN

This is not a film-set.
The skyline does not rise in the morning
Like the opening bars of *Rhapsody in Blue*,
And the taxi-driver at the lights at 74th and Broadway
Is not Travis Bickle;
The pigeons in Battery Park
Do not strut like the young Brando,
The couple arguing at the next table
Are not in a Woody Allen comedy,
And the mean streets of Little Italy
Don't mean what we think they should mean.

But in a bar in Greenwich Village
Between Ginsberg's apartment and Charlie Parker's house,
An Estonian football fan asks if we're from London;
When we explain that we're from the North of England
He frowns, and then laughs: '*Shameless*!'

CIDER IN THEIR EARS

in memory of Dave Sheasby

'the transformation of production under the sway of capital, means, at the same time, the martyrdom of the producer'
Marx

1

My text today's an Aesop Fable,
The one about the Country Mouse
Who left his plain provincial table
For some rich city cousin's house,
But finding rich food hard to swallow,
Ran straight back home. Conclusions follow
That those who cannot stand the pace
Should stay at home and know their place—
A moral that's designed to sweeten
A taste for life beyond the pale,
The backwoods, sticks, outside the whale,
While well-fed cats who come from Eton
Sleep purring dreams of sacrifice
And dine each night on country mice.

2

This tale was just a brief preamble—
I'm sorry that it took so long—
But sometimes poems need to ramble
To find the place where they belong.
I've only mentioned Aesop's creatures
Because I think that they might teach us
How easily we are consoled
To know that we've been undersold.
The virtues that we call Horatian
Like any wisdom, bear a price,
And this one's paid by more than mice:
Like education, education,
Old Labour, GONE, the BBC.
But more of that in Stanza 3.

3

The dictionary definition
Gives 'stanza' as 'a little room';
That's maybe why some composition
Can feel like writing with a broom
(Especially with my filthy scansion).
But every poem—if not a mansion—
Can be a well-built, lived in space
Where readers share *a sense of place*.
This was the title of a series
I made with Sheasby long ago,
In which we did our best to show
The North a place, and not a theory,
Society and art alive
Outside of the M25.

4

From Armitage to Zephaniah
Most poets write the way they speak;
But this verse—called *Onyeginskaya*
(My Russian accent's rather weak)—
Is neither chatty not informal,
The rhyme scheme's not exactly *normal*,
The bumpy engine's no Rolls Royce;
And yet I like this borrowed voice,
A public square whose architecture
Insists you get your head in shape—
Like listening to a Sheasby tape
(Or adult education lecture).
In short, I hope, the kind of poem
In which the reader feels at home.

5

Of course not every stanza's polished,
Sometimes the cracks begin to show,
Demanding that it be demolished—
Like that old house on Harrow Road,
A mansion which is now reduced to
(And this still takes some getting used to)
A block of swanky maisonettes.
Once home to wealthy Suffragettes,
And then to adult education,
This was a house that grew deep roots
Before the men in well-cut suits
Insisted on the separation
Of life and learning, town and gown.
Now fallen down, all fallen down.

6

Before the storm of market forces
Knocked down the walls of that old house
I used to teach there, evening courses;
One year, 'The Town and Country Mouse'
(ie *The Country and the City*);
The usual three-year Joint Committee
Tutorial Class; each week we'd race
Through writers with a sense of place,
Whose usages in English fiction—
From *Mansfield Park* to *Howard's End*—
Of England as a house, extend
In what seems now a valediction
To those who thought the gated wall
Of property might one day fall.

7

This 'Whim of Iron' (Dave's invention)
Swept through the Beeb. Now Radio Four's
All mini-ISAs, PEPS and pensions,
And *Money Box* and *You and Yours*,
And tax-advice for hedge-fund farmers,
And endless dull, Home Counties dramas,
The batsman walking to the crease,
Arts programmes made by press-release,
And comedies that just aren't funny...
But then if you're not from the smoke
The chances are, you'll miss the joke,
Like when the cut-glass voice of money
Cut Sheasby's tainted, awkward voice
And called the axe—*Producer Choice*.

8

But choosing doesn't mean you're chosen,
Belonging doesn't mean you're mute,
Being rooted doesn't mean you're frozen,
But radical (from *radix*, 'root').
These creatures talk of 'choice' and 'freedom'
(*The Moral Maze*) as though we need 'em,
As if the see-through walls of class
Weren't solid as the studio's glass.
The means—and meanings—of production
Expand with every choice we make,
And making them, are ours to take;
For harvest-mice (see Introduction)
The only happy ending's that
In which we learn to bell the cat.

On second thoughts, if that sounds Spartist,
I'll make the point in plainer ways:
Dave Sheasby was the kind of artist
Who lived in one house all his days.
The best art's made in confined spaces
By those who recognise their place is
Defined by things you *cannot* choose,
Just like an accent you can't use,
And being so, *is not diminished*;
The line that's drawn across the sand
Can deepen what we understand.
Three lines to go; I've almost finished;
Just time for one more rodent pun
Before these stanzas start to—run.

NO RUSH

for Maureen

after Martial Ep. V.10.

Best-selling verse, it's often said,
Sells best when written by the dead.
According to the apparatus
That gives dead authors classic status,
The world prefers to honour those
Who have begun to decompose,
While dead good writers are expected
To wait until they're safely dead
Before they see their works collected.
But who wants to be dead and read?
    As Martial put it (I'll translate)—
    Posterity can bloody wait.

BREATHLESS

in memory of Debbie

The day you rang I went out for a run,
    Your doctor's words still running round my head.
Outside, the fading February sun
    Was hanging in the hedgerows by a thread,
And what remained of day was grey and cold.
    But stopping at the top to get my breath
The sunset fields were filigreed with gold.

I hope the warmth between us at the death
    Was just enough to right where we went wrong,
But most I'm glad your spirit shone more bright
    As you grew weak, that illness made you strong,
That I have seen the way the dying light
    Illumines winter's leafless silhouettes,
And know the sun burns brightest as it sets.

BRILLIANT

for Geraldine, in memory of Paul

'*Je n'oublierai jamais le cortège les cris la foule et le soleil.*'
  Louis Aragon

The sun is out today, and so are we,
A sweaty host 800,000 strong
In a fair field of folk in Saint-Denis,
A *jacquerie* of poetry and song,
Warm solidarity, cold beer, hot food
From every nation underneath the sun.
Among this hot and bothered multitude
The world is wide enough for everyone.

For just one day the round earth seems complete,
Our common ends so brilliant and clear
In this uncommon, bright September weather;
A human planet dancing in the heat
Of comradeship. I'm glad that we are here,
But most of all, that we are here together.

Fête de l'Humanité, 2016

48

FORTY WINKS

for Pauline and Trevor

'*I'm not myself—I'm somebody else… everything's changed, and I'm changed,
and I can't tell what's my name, or who I am!*'
Washington Irving, *Rip Van Winkle*

1

My theme's that line by LP Hartley
About the passages of time;
No need to quote it fully (partly
Since *foreign country's* hard to rhyme).
But then, who hasn't had the notion
To run life backwards, in slow-motion,
Against the wind, rewind the tape?
We dream for decades of escape
Into a past that's ever fainter,
To put the clocks back, sail up-stream,
And find the source, as in a dream,
Jump ship, go sick and slip the painter
Like Rip Van Winkle's moonlight flit.
I have a dream—and *this* is it…

2

Although I'm not a great believer
In psychobabble, it's a dream
From which I wake up in a fever—
You know the one—in which you seem
To slip across that high-fenced border
Designed to keep the past in order,
And find yourself fifteen again,
And life a hazy regimen
Of homework, paper-rounds, *Daktari*,
Catullus and Subbuteo,
Tomorrow's World and Cicero,
The conjugations of *amare*,
And all the secrets clasped in bras—
More *Life on Earth* than *Life on Mars*.

3

But as the dream unfolds its story,
The midnight border-crossing shuts—
A classical *momento mori*
In which the film abruptly cuts,
And you're in bed, it's early morning,
Four decades skipped without a warning,
You've woken up in middle-age
And stand there naked on the stage;
You've lost the plot before it started,
You've fluffed your lines and missed your cue,
And don't know what you're meant to do
With all the things it seems you've bartered
For all the precious time you've spent,
And wonder where four decades went.

4

Four decades? Well, you do the numbers—
That's ten World Cups (or twice as long
As Rip Van Winkle's mountain slumbers).
Now yesterday is just a song
About regret. And no-one fancies
A decent bet on England's chances
Of victory in the *next* World Cup.
Perhaps the reels have got mixed up,
Or else you didn't pay attention
And missed the scene where you were told
That growing up means growing old
(*Before* you start to draw your pension)
Into a calm and wise old age
In which you're supposed to dress in *beige*.

5

For us the portrait in the attic
That stopped young Dorian going grey
Was shot on some old Instamatic—
Except it works the other way:
Our past lives are no laughing matter,
While they stay slim, we grow still fatter,
We frown while they keep smiling through,
Their black and white's our kind of blue,
Their bright ideas, our dull opinions.
They've seen the future on the screen
And think that it's a cross between
A Clockwork Orange and *St Trinian's*;
But we know how the movie ends—
Less *Peter Pan* than *Peter's Friends*.

6

Their crimes, of course, are undisputed,
A violent and eccentric cast
Of cartoon characters, more suited
To *If*, Greyfriars and *Gormenghast*—
Remote and terrifying creatures
(And that was just the kids!); the teachers
Had only bit-parts in the game
Of ritual cruelty and shame
We thought of as our adolescence.
Oh how we laughed! We nearly died!
They did their best, and though we tried
We could not fail to learn our lessons,
The ancient rules they made us learn
So we could fuck up in our turn.

7

We've had our fun; there's no mistaking
It's all downhill from this point on—
Like Rip Van Winkle who, on waking,
Discovered half his life was gone,
In middle-age we take our bearings
Between old hopes and new despairings,
While faithful Memory, old and blind,
Still dogs our heels, until we find
Our way back home illuminated
By breadcrumbs on a forest path
Or faces in a photograph.
Forget SatNavs—they're over-rated—
In order to get out alive
You need to catch the 215.

8

And if you do, give my best wishes
To all the ghosts I may have missed,
I'd really like to know how Fish is,
The laughing girl whom I once kissed.
They've not yet met (all that comes later)—
Where better than our *alma mater*
To teach them how to live in hope?
With love and friendship you can cope
No matter where the old bus takes us.
The future's always on its way;
The past however's here to stay.
We sleep for years, till something wakes us
Into a dream we seem to know
With friends from forty years ago…

FAIRY TALE

The future is a kitchen full of boxes,
An empty house, whose owners have just left;
We tip-toe through the rooms like Goldilockses,
Afraid that we might be accused of theft,
Or maybe that we've broken in to squat.
We make ourselves at home on chairs and beds
That are not ours. Inside the porridge pot
The future's slowly stirring in our heads.

My love, it's twenty years ago today
Since we first stepped together through the door
Of our own fairy-tale. Though far away
We sometimes still can hear the hungry roar
Of homeless fears come back to claim what's theirs,
We're safe and warm in here. The door's locked tight.
At night we hibernate like sleepy bears.
Our dreams are neither hard nor soft. Just right.

ASLEEP AT THE WHEEL

The children are asleep inside the van
And we are sitting underneath the stars,
Too tired to drive, so happy we can't speak.
If we're asleep, this dream is ours.

Five minutes more before we hit the road;
We share a can of flat and lukewarm beer.
Five hundred miles before we reach the coast;
But time's away, and we are here.

Your sleepy hand in mine, the speechless moon,
The warm French night, a last shared cigarette;
No matter what the miles ahead may bring,
This is as good as it can get.

We finish off the beer. Time we were off.
Your turn to get some kip, my turn to drive.
We've never felt so tired or so awake
As we are now, or so alive.

BOOKED

His hair is grey, though not with years,
His limbs are bowed, though not with toil,
His eyes are red, though not with tears,
His chamber lit by midnight oil,
A shadow of his former self—
A writer left upon the shelf.
Since books are written now by readers
Who may discover in the text
What those of us who write the bleeders
Do not intend, what follows next
Is that unless a book is read
It is (like modern authors) dead...

A spectre in the Stygian gloom
He drags his chains across the floor,
Awoken from the sleeping tomb
His ghostly slumbers are no more;
What nightmare stops his Lordship dozing?
The ghastly sound of bookshops closing.
Dead poets know their books are doomed
But in this electronic age
All writers find themselves consumed
On bonfires of the kindled page.
Dead poets unite! O shades of dread:
The wrath of the unread Undead!

Behold the spectres as they come,
All sex and drugs and *carmagnole*:
There's Wild Bill Blake on thund'ring drum,
And Coughing Johnny rock 'n' roll,
While every night 'Pete' Shelley's vocals
Are guaranteed to shock the locals.
In short, our ghostly host proposes
To take the band out on the road
(Think Ultravox meets Guns and Roses)—
The Ink Blots! How they once bestrode
All Europe with their art! He's sure
It's time they made a comeback tour.

Alas their plans are moving slowly;
There's two band members he can't find,
And without Dubya and Coaley
Their joy will not be unconfined.
But where have all the poets gone?
Like bookshops—up the Amazon.
In desperation they decide
To look in on an open mic.
Where public schoolboys who can't hide
The fact they don't really like
Unchilled white wine ('it isn't done!')
Recite the prizes they have won.

They search the supermarket shelves
In vain—no sign of poets there!
Too late our heroes see themselves
Reflected in the brain-dead stare
Of some pale shadow off his trolley;
Too late our heroes see their folly,
They turn to run, the zombie screams,
The other shoppers chase the gang
Down to the river, where it seems
They're trapped. But then a nasal twang
Drifts o'er the waves: 'Now then, young man,
If I can't help you, no-one can.'

He leads the way across the Trent—
'I told them I could walk on water…'
The zombies though, are still intent
On putting poets to the slaughter,
'In here!' They slip inside a new shop
(At least it's not another shoe-shop)
And try to barricade the door,
Hang on a minute—what's this place?
A well-stocked bookshop! What is more,
The clones have given up the chase,
Here's Dubya signing books, and there
Is Coaley (looking worse for wear).

A softly spoken Scot explains,
'They can't get in, so never fear,
As long as we still use our brains.'
'You mean?' 'That's right, we're Luddites here.'
At which, their lordships get excited:
'Book lovers of the world united!'
They rabbit on, as Big'eds should,
'We will die fighting, or live free,
And down with all kings but King Ludd!'
And as they finish, all can see
They're both made of the self-same stuff:
A two-for-one deal—Byron Clough!

These days dead poets can be found
On wet and windy Saturdays—
The subs' bench at the City Ground.
The Boss, of course, decides who plays,
But sometimes when the Forest's tired,
He knows their ghostly help's required—
A tackle here, a well-timed pass,
A useful rhyme, a hero's name,
A common goal, a dream of grass;
Dead poets know how to read the game
And if they do not win promotion
It's always *poetry in motion*…

DON AND DONNA

for Insy and in memory of Jacquesy

'... He's as far
From the enjoyment of the earth and air
Who watches o'er the chain, as they who wear.'
Byron, *Don Juan*

I

I do not want a hero may not sound
    The most dramatic way to start this Canto,
But since this is a song (the word is found
    In Latin, Spanish, French and Esperanto),
I want to strike a note that's less profound,
    More suitable to circus ring or panto;
It's hard to play Mariah Carey's *Hero,*
Or *Rocky III*—then introduce a Pierrot.

II

I can't, you see, join in the world's obsession
    With caped crusaders, X-Men and the like
Whose deeds are used to justify aggression
    (Like fearless Siegfried in the old Third Reich),
And since we're in a Double-dip Recession
    I'd rather trust a Chaplin or a Svejk
To understand the world of economics
Than someone in a mask from Marvell Comics.

III

A hero's job's to keep us entertained,
    Or failing that, to keep the masses quiet,
A spectacle of violence unrestrained
    Reminding us it doesn't pay to riot;

So Law and Order's properly maintained,
    They force-feed us a bread and circus diet
Which we must chew for hour after hour
(Just like a box-set featuring Jack Bauer).

IV

Meanwhile real life's a bitch, an old Rottweiler
    Which disapproves of thinking in the ranks—
A Sampson found in Gaza with Delilah
    Would be run over by Israeli tanks,
A street-wise Hercules (*viz* Bonnie Tyler)
    Would be defeated by the Augean banks,
And Chagos Islanders now realise
Exactly where and how real power lies.

V

Although ours is an unheroic Age,
    The ancient want of heroes is still fed
By paladins of pitch and screen and stage,
    Whose epic labours in the bar and bed
Are bared upon the naked tabloid page
    So we can worship them *before* they're dead.
(Mortality being better left to plebs,
Elysium's now exclusive to celebs.)

VI

Their virtues on a greater scale than ours,
    Our pin-ups strive to be the Very Best,
Endowed by us with all the super-powers
    We used to think that only gods possessed—
Until, alas, the faithless world devours
    Mistakes that even tabloids can't digest.
We've barely hung the icons on the wall
Before we have to watch our heroes fall.

VII

Rebekah Brookes, Bob Diamond, Liam Fox!
　　How soon it seems the heroes of today
Are swept on fickle tides towards the rocks.
　　François Hollande, James Murdoch, DSK!
Each in their turn paraded in the stocks
　　That all the world can see their feet of clay.
How quickly reputations all unravel,
From Cameron and Clegg to Jimmy Saville.

VIII

So brief and thankless is a hero's span!
　　You only need a small illegal war
To flush a Bush or Straw straight down the pan,
　　Their reputations washed away before
Diogenes could find an honest man.
　　It seems the world prefers the kind of flaw
Or *hamartia* (q.v. Aristotle)
That strips a hero down to cock and bottle.

IX

Undone by careless tweet and casual text
　　The old heroic lay is tuneless now;
John Terry! Ashley Cole! Whoever next?
　　Ah Signor Berlusconi—take a bow!
Although the rich may think they're over-sexed
　　It only takes a wig and botox-brow
To give the rest of us a little chortle
And let us know our heroes are still mortal.

X

First Ronan Keating, Sven and Gen. Petraus,
    Then Ryan Giggs, Chris Huhne and Cyril Smith—
Our idols seem determined to betray us
    (Straight after they've betrayed their kin and kith);
We slowly peel the weeping onion layers
    Until there's nothing left but tears and pith.
To make an ageing Alpha-male look younger
Requires more than a bit of *bunga bunga*.

XI

I'm sure that being a hero isn't easy,
    And fame can be mistaken for success;
A winning smile can soon become too cheesy,
    A pious frown can also look like stress,
And clever clogs make everyone feel queasy,
    Especially when they fall for their own press.
Of course I know it's all been said before—
But there are no Shakespearoes anymore.

XII

One day we hail them as the new Messiah,
    The next, their names are trampled in the dust;
Ingratitude and jealousy conspire
    Until a god like Tony Blair seems just
An orange-faced, transparent, venal liar
    Whom nobody with any brains would trust.
But then we like our heroes on their arses,
Especially when they're from the *apper clarsses*.

XIII

To every fallen hero it must seem
    The fawning world's turned suddenly ungrateful—
One minute they're a TV chat-show dream
    The next their twitter feeds are simply *hateful.*
One night they get to lick—ahem—the cream
    Then wake to find they've had a tabloid plateful.
Each in their turn like Banquo's monarchs stalk;
They talked the talk, and now they have to walk.

XIV

A Byron trying to swim the Hellespont,
    A Hero waiting for her own Leander,
A posh cunt in a punt without a quant,
    The chances of a fuck if you're a panda—
Confusing what you need with what you want
    Is typical Romantic propaganda,
A schoolboy error. Yet it doth appear
To be the reason why we're all in here.

XV

In here? You mean to say you haven't guessed?
    My fault. I thought you'd recognise the smells
Of polish, fags and chips and all the rest,
    The hollow halls, with sparry roofs and cells.
In other words, like me, you're now a guest
    Of Her Britannic Majesty's hotels:
Which one is not important for our tale,
The point is that this Canto's set in gaol.

XVI

I'd like to give you all a guided tour,
    (You must hand in your mobiles at the Gate);
Alas, this is quite contrary to the Law
    That says a man must be prepared to wait
For twenty hours a day behind his door,
    Reduced unto a space 12 foot by 8.
And if this gives our tale a narrowed view,
I hope such limits make it ring more true.

XVII

Because I'm not allowed to show you round
    You'll have to let me tell you what I know,
And since I'm buried six feet under ground
    I'm going to have to tell instead of show;
I know this is a heresy that's frowned
    Upon by critics everywhere you go,
But I would rather trust in my own eyes
To perfect knowledge of the boundless skies.

XVIII

If you want heroes, gaol's the place to be.
    They're at the windows, Bang-up to Unlock;
There's plastic gangsters down on Houseblock 3,
    And YPs swinging batteries in a sock,
There's blokes from EDL and BNP,
    And would-be Charlie Bronsons down the Block,
And Muslim lads who think they look Jihadist.
And each, of course, believes that they're the *baddest*.

XIX

They're not bad lads though, most of them in here,
    A few not right inside their heads, perhaps;
Too many have been too long on the gear
    And ricochet from rehab to relapse;
Too many raised in poverty and fear,
    Too few have ever tasted more than scraps.
A warehouse full of damaged minds and bodies—
And that's before we talk about the squaddies.

XX

We send them out to Helmland and Iraq
    Just like when half the globe was coloured red,
Then guiltily we fly the bodies back;
    Not quite a hero's welcome, but instead
A coffin wrapped inside a Union Jack.
    We call them heroes when they're safely dead,
But there's now twice as many in the can
As there are serving in Afghanistan.

XXI

The screws, meanwhile, are from the self-same mould,
    Same class, same towns, same football teams, same wars;
But something in the way the dice were rolled
    Means they go home when we're behind our doors;
They warm themselves at night; our nights are cold;
    And while penologists debate the cause,
We keep them in employment; our mistakes
Are just the flip-side of their lucky breaks.

XXII

A thousand men banged-up from dusk to dawn
　　　Is not, by anybody's definition,
A happy place to be; there's no man born
　　　Can flourish in this sunless, dull condition
Illumined only by the grey of morn
　　　(As if the penny-pinching Coalition
Condemned the day before it had begun,
To pacify the readers of the *Sun*).

XXIII

The lowest of the low, you see, that's us.
　　　The outcasts, outlaws, losers out and in,
Our punishment gives other folk a buzz,
　　　We have to lose so other folk can win;
And yet we know—if anybody does—
　　　That we're all brothers underneath the skin.
The day you get to walk out through the Gate,
Your pad's filled by some lad from your estate.

XXIV

It's not a *choice* to sit here, years on end,
　　　There's not a man inside who doesn't miss
The warmth of lover, parent, child and friend,
　　　There's no-one *wants* to spend their time like this;
And just because there's some lads who pretend
　　　Incarceration is a piece of piss,
It doesn't mean that prison makes you tougher;
The more you say you don't, the more you suffer.

XXV

Which doesn't mean that everybody's blameless,
 Or prison is a bad idea *per se*;
We may look like we're from the cast of *Shameless,*
 Unlucky, stupid, hopeless, you might say,
But most are here because our lives are aimless,
 And not because we planned to live this way.
No matter if you think you don't deserve it,
Be wary, watch the time, and always serve it.

XXVI

We're prisoners here of more than our own Fate,
 Combatants in an economic war
In which the forces of the modern State
 Are used to discipline the jobless poor
By offering us a choice of Going Straight
 Or years spent learning How to Mop a Floor.
I know, I know, you probably think I'm shitting,
But that's the way it looks from where I'm sitting.

XXVII

A cheap supply of labour—that's our job,
 To undercut the pay of those outside.
No unions here, of course. The bastards rob
 You blind then sell you back your one good eye;
Between the dole queue and the tabloid mob,
 The Market and the Law in gaol collide.
We've seen the future and it doesn't pay.
A prisoner works for 80p a day.

XXVIII

For anyone who's stuck inside the whale
    When you wake up you know your head's in shreds;
Like Charon's bark of spectres, dull and pale,
    We shuffle down the Wing to get our meds,
To help us through another day in gaol,
    Another lonely day inside our heads,
Deciding to be bored or to be boring.
Who wouldn't rather spend the whole day snoring?

XXIX

From friends, and home, and freedom far estranged,
    A crowd of shivering slaves of every nation.
Poor bastards! Youth's good looks are sadly changed
    By years of ultra-violet deprivation;
One half denied, the other half deranged,
    All save the black lads, jaded with vexation;
The poorest, more philosophy display,
They're used to this, as bankers to their pay.

XXX

One morning I was cleaning on the 2s,
    When in walks this young lad with all his kit
Escorted by the usual pair of Screws.
    A new arrival usually looks like shit,
But this one was a cross between Tom Cruise
    Jake Gyllenhaal, Tom Hardy and Brad Pitt;
A lot more Charlie Brown than Charlie Bronson.
Apparently his name was Donald Johnson.

XXXI

The lads on B Wing liked him straight away,
    He had what you might call a moonshine smile;
What was he in for? Donny wouldn't say.
    'A crime,' he'd shrug (remorse was not his style).
Somebody thought to call the boy DJ
    Because he'd worked the decks on some Greek isle;
The club—run by a very special lady—
Before it was shut down, was called *The Haidée*.

XXXII

He was a proper ladeez man, was Don;
    He had them writing letters from all over;
He stuck their photos up, a real Don Juan
    Our Donny was, a right old Casanova,
His talent was to turn the lasses on
    (Then turn 'em off) from Aberdeen to Dover;
In short, the kind of bloke who thinks his duty's
To pleasure all of Albion's female beauties.

XXXIII

Although regarding other people's wives
    He could have been a little more discreet,
I doubt he was the sort of bloke who thrives
    On playing games of marital deceit;
Bur randy cats like that have several lives
    And Donny always landed on his feet.
In short, it seemed that this cat wasn't fussy
As long as he was never short of pussy.

XXXIV

Which brings me to the next part of our drama.
　　A few weeks later we were down the Gym;
While Donny's biceps bulged like body armour
　　At my age I was running to stay slim,
While he moved with the grace of an Obama
　　I felt the years in every weary limb.
You do your time, but time keeps marching on.
One day your life's before you. Then it's gone.

XXXV

Time marches on, and yet all prisoners know
　　How slow the grains of sand fall through the glass,
Some days it seems the minutes go so slow
　　You almost hear the ticking decades pass.
Perhaps that's why I said that I would go
　　With Don to the Creative Writing Class
With *cups of tea* (the usual prison bribery)
Beginning Wednesday morning in the library.

XXXVI

O ye, who make your fortunes writing books!
　　Remember those who tend the temple flame
In prison libraries. *O fiat lux!*
　　They get so little thanks and so much blame
For trying to help a bunch of cons and crooks
　　Find out about the world from which we came,
Or failing that, to find upon these shelves
The words with which to speak about ourselves.

XXXVII

As somebody once said, 'all poets steal'
 And every prison's full of thieves turned writers;
Confinement makes the need to write more real,
 And lads who in their normal lives are fighters
In prison want to write down how they feel.
 Though some may think this kind of art detritus,
It's infinitely preferable to
The shit they print in *Poetry Review*.

XXXVIII

So many prizes and so little art!
 For those whose lives are cabin'd, cribb'd, confined,
Nobody ever needs to set apart
 The dancer from the dance; art's not designed
To elevate the lucky and the smart
 But to remind us what we share in kind,
And that this lonely world's not always friendless.
Though Art is brief, in prison Life is endless.

XXXIX

I don't know what we thought we might achieve,
 But by next week twelve lads had put in apps—
Two rappers and a Byron-fan called Steve,
 Four nature poets, a vampire buff, two saps
Who though it was calligraphy (believe!)
 Plus me and Don—a dozen wary chaps
And one of our Creative Writing tutors,
Sat like Penelope among her suitors.

XL

A poet—Spoken Word Performer *please*!
 (She saw herself as one who broke the mould)—
She'd slammed at raves and rapped with grime MCs,
 Her Glasto set last year was download gold,
Her blog about the plight of Burmese bees
 Went viral overnight (the rights were sold
To Channel 4), meanwhile her pamphlet *Voice*
Was this month's Poetry Book Society Choice.

XLI

Her debut album with The Useless Fucks
 Had earned her much acclaim and several prizes—
It said so on the back of both her books
 (As slim as Donna was)—but my surmise is
The judges were acquainted with her looks;
 Though talent comes in many shapes and sizes,
Success is rarely given to the plain,
And woman's face was never form'd in vain.

XLII

She told us that she was a great believer
 In writers who interrogate taboo,
Waxed lyrical of Wilde and Eldridge Cleaver,
 Un Prophète, Dostoevsky and Camus,
And worked herself into a right old fever
 While reading from a book by you know who.
God knows why she was telling us this stuff,
But when she talked we couldn't get enough.

XLIII

This woman was (but how should I describe
    Her virtues?) of the overpowering kind;
Unless some beauty with a kiss should bribe,
    I'd say most men grow old and never find
So rare a model of the tender tribe,
    So perfect for the onanistic mind.
O Love! How perfect is thy mystic art!
And how deceitful is the sagest heart!

XLIV

Of course once news of Donna got about
    The apps came pouring in. The following week
The place was packed. So many years without
    A lovely female face makes strong men weak.
And Donna had a face, without a doubt;
    It seemed her conscious heart glowed in her cheek,
And we began to feel, in every lecture,
More *Cool Hand Luke* than Norman Stanley Fletcher.

XLV

Each week we bared our souls for her to read
    (And in return we'd mentally undress her);
We poured our bleeding hearts out by the screed,
    If we were sinners, she was our confessor,
And yet we somehow knew we'd not succeed—
    Our sentences seemed only to depress her—
She said she wanted something darker, *raw*,
Transgressive nature red in tooth and claw.

XLVI

Her answer was to hold a Poetry Slam,
    That *Vade Mecum* of the true sublime,
Where vanity competes with bad Am Dram
    And every joke's delivered with a rhyme.
Some started cramming as for an exam
    While others started rhyming all the time,
Perhaps believing there's some urban glamour
To be obtained while slamming in the Slammer.

XLVII

The day arrived at last. The place was heaving.
    The mood was tense. The poets, though rehearsed,
Were nervous as before a night of thieving;
    Each meant to do their best (or do their worst),
Each dry-mouthed author hoping and believing
    That they might win the prize and come in first.
While, wise and cunning as Minerva's Owl,
Sat Donna in the role of Simon Cowell.

XLVIII

The thin white rappers rapped and slapped their bitches,
    The Nature poets sang their Nonny Nonny,
The vampire moaned about some Gothic witches,
    The Stand-ups stood up, then sat down, while Donny
Had everybody in the room in stitches
    With something borrowed straight from *Purple Ronnie*;
When my turn came I stared into my coffee,
Because—alas—I cannot write for toffee.

XLIX

Last up was Steve the Byron fan, first seen
    In stanza 39, with some new lay
About the current economic scene—
    Which prospect filled the audience with dismay
(I should explain, Steve was a cross between
    Andreas Baader, Malcolm X and Che).
But if not Orpheus quite, when Greece was young,
He sang, or would, or could, or should have sung:

***

The trials of Greece, the trials of Greece!
    Where noble Byron loved and sung,
Now suicidal rates increase
    Among the jobless Attic young;
Eternal summer gilds them yet,
But all, except their sun, is debt.

Dictatorship and civil war,
    A US-bankrolled Fascist coup,
Could not achieve what EU law
    And international banks now do;
For Greeks a blush, for Greece a tear.
For tourists, dearer *Mythos* beer.

The harp's unstrung, the lute is mute.
    The dream that Greece might still be free
Is lost on those in hot pursuit
    Of sun and sex and sand and sea,
Who only want to dance till morn
And chill out in the Golden Dawn.

As likely send a prayer to Isis
    As hope that we might fight the greed
Of those who caused the Euro Crisis;
    Europa bullied does not need
Another despot of this kind;
Such chains as these are sure to bind.

What, silent still? And silent all?
    The isles of Greece are held in thrall
Because we did not heed the call
    Inscribed upon the Doric wall,
Ευρώπη ξεσηκώσου!
(*Europe Arise! Europe Arise!*)

***

L

He stopped abruptly, blushing as our Muse,
    The blessed Donna, opened her critique
By saying it was very hard it was choose
    Between so many talents—even Greek!
(Steve blushed again.) Though poets should enthuse,
    She said they should be *sassy, dark, oblique.*
Steve blushed again with pleasure, whereupon
She said the champion Slammer was—our Don.

LI

And that was when the trouble started brewing.
    While Donny did his best to hide a smirk,
The Goth went pale, the Stand-ups started booing,
    The rappers flapped and yapped about their work,
It sounded like the Georgian poets were mooing,
    And Steve appeared about to go berserk;
At which point Donna, seeing what she'd started,
Decided it was time that she departed.

LII

Next thing we knew, they'd closed the Writing Group
    And Steve was nicked (which seemed a tad unjust),
While Donna, who was clearly in the soup,
    Had promptly vanished in a cloud of dust,
Thus leaving us, who cannot fly the coop
    As easily as that, somewhat nonplussed.
Next thing we knew, they gave Don his Cat D,
And with one bound the cat was—almost—free.

LIII

What happened next is anybody's guess.
    Time spent inside an open prison's not
The holiday imagined by the press;
    Put one foot wrong, you're back in like a shot.
Some fail because they just can't stand the stress,
    At least in here you're left alone to rot.
In short, the odds on his return were long.
But obviously we got old DJ wrong.

LIV

A few months later, sitting in my pad,
    I'm writing letters with my telly on
(No word from Donald Johnson, I might add,
    Though many men fall silent once they've gone).
First *News at Ten*, some ads, then *Mad 'n' Bad*
    A late-night arts show featuring—our Don!
And drop-dead Donna, looking like a dream.
Both purring like the cats that got the cream.

LV

He sat there like a very naughty kitten
 While Donna talked about *The Awesome Fleece*,
A hip-hop opera which they'd just co-written
 For this year's Byron festival in Greece;
While Tony Parsons was 'completely smitten'
 And Jay-Z called the work 'a masterpiece',
Mark Lawson said he thought this new libretto
Was W.H. Auden meets the Ghetto.

LVI

It seemed that Don—our Don!—had struck it rich
 Since he got out; the boy was now rebranded
As Don-Catraz, a new persona which,
 As ludicrous as it was less than candid,
No doubt would prove to be a useful pitch
 For *Guardian* critics. Looked like Don had landed
With both feet on the ground, 'a modern Rimbaud'
Dressed up to look like Tupac and/or Rambo.

LVII

Of course the boy was always rather dapper,
 He had the Jack the Lad good looks in spades,
But now they'd dressed him up just like a rapper
 In baggy trousers, hoodie, trainers, shades,
An outsize trucker-cap upon his nappa,
 His hair in geometric cornrow braids;
As innocent as Rousseau's *Bon Sauvage,*
The handsome Caliban who made it large:

***

The aisles of Greece, the aisles of Greece!
　　It's time to party with the Don
And celebrate the boy's release,
　　So hit the dance-floor, get it on,
Cos when you're really off your tree,
The deejay makes a cool emcee.

I'll get you dancing in the aisles
　　On Kavos, Kos and Ayia Nappa,
A crowd of blissed-out aceed smiles
　　Because I is a well sick Rapper,
A toke, a drink, a pill, a line,
Fill high the cup with Samian wine!

From midnight till the sun comes up
　　The virgins dance beneath the shade,
While awkward heroes stand and sup
　　And gaze upon each glowing maid
Competing in the Pyrrhic dances,
And try to calculate their chances.

The Scian and the Teian muse
　　Are in the toilets, selling dope;
Heroic bosoms, soaked in booze,
　　Are caught in poses which they hope
Will decorate their Facebook page,
To prove that they have come of age.

Behold his lordship on the decks!
　　The dance-floor packed with kids on eez
Who come to Greece for Club Med sex
　　And pick up nasty STDs
To sounds which echo further west,
Then back to uni for a rest.

***

LVIII

To tell the truth, the boy had always seemed
    Not quite the brightest monkey in the lab,
But judging by the way they whooped and screamed
    When Donny did his krumping street-dance jab,
He'd somehow morphed himself (or was he memed?)
    To something which the world now thought was fab,
He always was the luckiest of fellers,
But all the same, I can't say I was jealous.

LIX

Soon Don and Donna were a tabloid item
    To rival Brad and Jen or Pete and Katie;
Their Tweets were twittered fast as they could write 'em,
    Their plans to build an orphanage on Haiti
Were splashed in *Bitch* and *Knobz*, *ad infinitum.*
    In short, the world was so pleased they were matey
That, after cloying the gazettes with cant,
Don hinted that his Donna was *enceinte.*

LX

Alas, their happy tale had just begun
    When next we heard she'd hit him for a six
(You probably saw the photos in the *Sun*);
    It seemed she'd caught him up to his old tricks
And when she found out what the boy had done,
    Poor Donna dropped him like a ton of bricks.
But then good scandals make the press a blessing,
Especially if you're photographed undressing.

LXI

Soon after that Don disappeared from view.
 The tabloid trail went cold. They'd better phones
To hack, and more vendettas to pursue.
 No doubt he's off exploring other zones
Erogenous and warm, in pastures new;
 The world out there is full of Donna clones
Who in a tender, moonlight situation
Will disregard a hero's reputation.

LXII

Meanwhile, the lads on B Wing are still here
 And every day's as pointless as the last.
The passing of another useless year
 Reminds us that we're going nowhere fast—
Except the pockets of the privateer
 Who's bought all the dead souls in this *oblast*.
The surest way to profit from austerity
Is passing on the invoice to posterity.

LXIII

O Time! Why must thou pause? Take up thy sickle!
 How long before we wake to see the light?
For any length of days in such a pickle
 A man must soon become an eremite;
The sand inside the glass slows to a trickle
 When you're locked in a toilet day and night.
In order to placate the tabloid editors,
They feed us to the privatising predators.

LXIV

Hark! Through the silence of the cold, dull night,
    The hum of prisons gather rank on rank
To keep us out of mind and out of sight:
    Ten million human beings in the tank
On this poor planet. Sold without a fight.
    Trust not for freedom to the merchant bank.
The truth is that the truth won't set you free;
So when it doesn't, don't come blaming me.

LXV

For if I've bent the truth, or botched my rhymes,
    It clearly wasn't done for bloody payment.
These days I'm sure that there are greater crimes
    (An extra bedroom when you're still a claimant
Will get you on the front-page of *The Times*).
    And since there are no angels in bright raiment
We need (and please don't think I'm being satirical)
A revolution—or a fucking miracle.

LXVI

Inside or out, we haven't got a hope.
    Between CCTV and IPP
Our freedom's on a short and slippery slope;
    And though they like to tell you that you're free
This goes for you as well; your longer rope
    Allows you just the freedom to agree
The liberties they take are justified.
And if you don't, there's room for you inside.

LXVII

Though governments in our time like to claim
 That every year the crime statistics fall,
The public still needs somebody to blame,
 As though behind each breezeblock prison wall
The public tries to hide their private shame
 At how our liberties were sold, how all
The nations are in prison, behind bars
That circumscribe your world as much as ours.

EFTALOU

for John at 80

Roll on, thou deep and dark blue Ocean—roll!
Ten thousand dinghies perished here in vain,
Their frail and freighted flotsam swallowed whole
With bubbling groan. Now nothing doth remain
To mark the earth with ruin; the salt demesne
Which guards this pebbled strand has washed away
Each death as if it were a drop of rain,
A tear soon drowned among the waves' wild play.
Such as creation's dawn beheld, thou roll'st today.

Assyria, NATO, Carthage, EU, Rome—
Unceasing as the seas that beat these shores
And violent as the thunder in the foam,
The empire of the whale has closed its jaws
On those made homeless by its endless wars.
Weighed down by so much reckless hope, they told
Their desperate stories to the sea's applause,
Until the tide of tv cameras rolled
Away, and stranger, slave or savage, all were sold.

DOODGESKIET

in memory of Chris Hani

Last night I dreamed I saw the man
Who murdered Comrade B,
Says I, 'you should be twelve months dead.'
'I never died,' says he,
'I never died,' says he.

'In 1993,' says I,
Him standing by my bed,
'They gaoled you on a murder charge.'
Says he, 'but I ain't dead,'
Says he, 'but I ain't dead.'

'Democracy imprisoned you,
We locked you up,' says I.
'Takes more than votes to kill a man,'
Says he, 'I didn't die,'
Says he, 'I didn't die.'

And standing there as big as life
And smiling with his eyes
He says, 'what they forgot to kill
Went on to organize,
Went on to organize.

'They promised you the coming Dawn,
But promises come cheap—
We bought your dreams of liberty
While you were still asleep,
While you were still asleep.

'From Boksburg up to Guptagate,
 In every mine and mill,
Where working people stand and fight,'
 Says he, 'you'll find me still,'
 Says he, 'you'll find me still.

 Last night I dreamed I saw the man
Who murdered Comrade B,
 Says I, 'you should be twelve months dead.'
'I never died,' says he,
'I never died,' says he.

THE COSMONAUTS OF ULM

'Der Mensch ist kein Vogel'
Brecht

When the Bishop told the waiting crowds
That the tailor was quite dead,
The crowd began to sing and dance with mirth;
'We knew he'd never fly,' they said,
'His head was in the clouds,
And now his pride has brought him down to earth.'

They left the tailor where he lay
Upon the broken stones,
So nobody would try to fly again;
His broken wings and broken bones
Reminders to obey
The heavy laws of gravity and men.

And so the world goes spinning by,
And upstart stars still fall,
Beneath our heavy boots the planet clings;
And only bird-brains still recall
How we once tried to fly
Around the broken earth on gorgeous wings.

NOTES

The Sailors of Ulm
This poem is based on MacNeice's 'Thalassa'. The title refers to Bertolt Brecht's poem 'The Tailor of Ulm' and to Lucio Magri's history of the Italian Communist Party, *Il Sarto di Ulm*.

The Great Bell in Martín Espada's Chest
This poem is based on a health scare suffered by the US/Puerto Rican poet Martín Espada when he was reading in the UK, shortly after he had translated Adrian Mitchell's 'The Great Bell in Paul Robeson's Chest' into Spanish.

The Apollo Pavilion
The Apollo Pavilion (1970) is a piece of public art in Peterlee, Co Durham, designed by Victor Pasmore and made of reinforced concrete.

Moving Backwards
The title refers to the phrase 'Moving Forward' in Middlesbrough Borough Council's current logo (which itself echoes the town's motto *Erimus*, or 'we shall be'). It also references *Looking Backward* (1880), a socialist utopian novel by the US writer Edward Bellamy (1850–1898). In *The Republic* Plato described lyric poetry as springing like a fountain from a pool. Ian Stubbs is a Middlesbrough historian and formerly the Assistant Curator of the Dorman Museum. In *The Inferno* the gate of Hell bears an inscription which ends, '*Lasciate ogne speranza, voi ch'intrate*', or 'Abandon hope, all you who enter here'. The architect Phillip Webb (1831–1915) was a partner in William Morris's Company; he designed the (now vacant) Middlesbrough offices of Bell & Co on Zetland Road. Middlesbrough's original town hall was painted by LS Lowry in 1959. In 1862 William Gladstone addressed a meeting in the old town hall, famously describing Middlesbrough as 'an infant Hercules'. Until its closure in 2010, the Captain Cook was one of the oldest surviving public houses in the town. Local legend says that Peg Powler is a green-toothed witch who lives in the River Tees. In the third series of *Auf*

Weidersehen Pet (2002) the Transporter Bridge is demolished and rebuilt in Arizona.

The Work of Giants

Prior Park, in Combe Down, near Bath, was built in 1742 by John Wood for Ralph Allen, the founder of the pre-privatised British postal service and the model for Squire Allworthy in *Tom Jones*. Harry Patch was born in Combe Down. Frederic Weatherly (who wrote the words to the song 'Danny Boy') lived in the village before the First World War. The 1953 Ealing comedy *The Titfield Thunderbolt* was filmed in Combe Down.

Tomskaya Pisanitsa

A few miles outside Kemerovo in Siberia, Tomskaya Pisanitsa Park is famous for a series of Neolithic rock-carvings on the banks of the river Tom. Alexei Leonov, the first human to walk in space, was born in Kemerovo. *Comrade One-Crutch* is the title of a children's novel by the US writer Ruth Epperson Kennell set in Kemerovo in the 1920s. Bear Rock Cave is south of Kemerovo in the Altai Krai, the site of the recent discovery of 'Woman X' or the 'Denisova Hominin'.

archy says hooray

'archy' is the slow-typing cockroach who featured in Don Marquis' column in the New York *Evening Sun* in the 1910s and 1920s.

A Willimantic Fable

The incident of the frogs is said to have taken place in Willimantic, Connecticut in 1754.

Cider in their Ears

GONE was the acronym of Government North East until it was abolished in 2011.

Booked

This poem uses several lines from Byron's *The Prisoner of Chillon*.

Don and Donna
This poem was written while working at HMPs Moorland and Lindholme in South Yorkshire.

Eftalou
The beach at Eftalou on northern Lesvos is where the Syrian refugees arrived by sea from the Turkish mainland in early 2015. This poem borrows several lines, as well as the Spenserian stanza, from Byron's *Childe Harold* Canto IV.

Doodgeskiet
Chris Hani was the general secretary of the South African Communist Party and chief of staff of Umkhonto we Sizwe (the armed wing of the ANC). He was murdered in Boksburg in 1993. 'Doodgeskiet' means 'dead' in Afrikaans; Comrade B was Hani's name inside Umkhonto we Sizwe. The poem is, of course, based on the old IWW song 'Joe Hill'.

The Cosmonauts of Ulm
In 1978 the East German cosmonaut Sigmund Jähn became the first German to fly into space. He took with him a toy figure of the *Sandmännchen*. Based on Hans Christian Andersen's character *Ole Lukøje*, the Little Sandman who brings dreams to children was a popular animated character on GDR television.